D1707394

12 THESES ON ATTENTION

authored by

The Friends of Attention

D. Graham Burnett and Stevie Knauss, eds.

The Friends of Attention

in conjunction with

Princeton University Press
Princeton, NJ

Published by The Friends of Attention
friendsofattention.net
with the support of The Institute for Sustained Attention,
a non-profit organization

Distributed by
Princeton University Press
41 William Street
Princeton, NJ 08540
press.princeton.edu

Library of Congress Control Number: 2021953069
ISBN: 978-0-691-23982-8
British Library Cataloguing-in-Publication data is available

This book has been composed in Sofia Pro and Neue Haas Grotesk

Printed in the United Kingdom

10 9 8 7 6 5 4 3 2 1

At other times when I hear the wind blow
I feel just hearing the wind blow makes it worth being born.

I don't know what others will think when they read this;
But I think it must be good because I think it without effort...

FERNANDO PESSOA

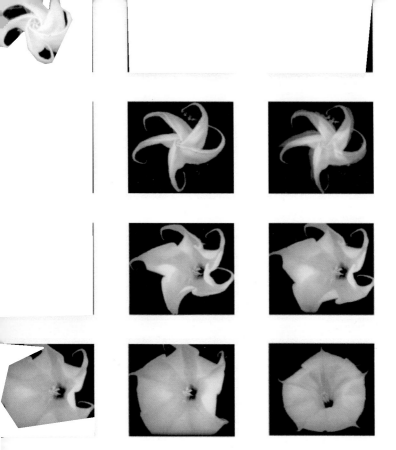

INTRODUCTION

Survival is itself difficult. To thrive and flourish, with others — this is the hope. Therefore, when and as we are able, we must work for this (and play, too, for this).

This small book has been composed by a group of friends — real friends, who are also "Friends." The collaborators are all linked with the "Friends of Attention," a gentle coalition of activists, artists, and others who cultivate, theorize, and share forms of attention *resistant to commodification*.

What does this mean? It means that the Friends (who found each other over the years, through creative work and writing and study and collaboration) are committed to "attention" in a special way. In fact, as we try to say in the pages that follow, we believe that radical human attention unfolds the astonishing reality of the world. And we believe, further, that this kind of unfolding is no decadent privilege. Rather, we think it is fundamental to the goodness of life, and therefore, properly, belongs to all as an essential and enabling good.

These THESES have been written by people who believe this, and who hold this belief on the basis of diverse, intimate, individual, and collective experiences of radical attention — of the ways it can transform, deepen, bind, and enchant. From such experiences has arisen their Friendship. And from such experiences has arisen their desire to find new friends in this shared good — a good which may be the good of goods, and which is, in the end, not even scarce. It is available to all, and near at hand. We need only attend.

That said, we worry. And we have written these pages because we worry. New and rapidly changing conditions threaten the forms of attention we care about most, and upon which we place our hopes. Like many others, we fear the rise of a powerful new financial, commercial, and technological system that is commodifying human attention as never before (turning it into a thing to be bought and sold). This new economy, operating at a scale and on channels previously unimaginable, has created — is creating — increasingly impossible conditions for the cultivation and practice of the forms of attention we believe make life good (that console us when we suffer, arm us against loneliness and despair, and set the conditions of suffusing joy).

Are we right in what we say here below? We aren't sure. The Friends of Attention make drafts — no finished texts. So treat what follows as a work-in-progress. There is a fair bit of whitespace in these pages. Feel free to fill it in. Add your own thoughts. If you like, send them our way. Help us understand. The work of understanding is the work of care. Which is itself the work of attention. Like friendship.

And one can never have too many Friends.

I.

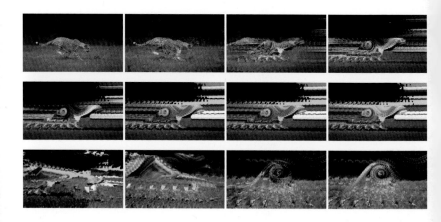

The astonishing reality of things, beings, and persons —
this is the object of pure attention.

2.

II.

True attention does the work of *bringing forth.*
It is the aperture through which the latency of things,
beings, and persons becomes present.

"Mere" attention, ordinary attentiveness, is *useful,*
standing in relation to the world like the opening,
closing, entering, and exiting of the sensible doors in
a well-maintained house.

But unmixed attention — pure attention to what cannot be used, to what no one already wants, to what promises no knowledge or gain — does not require doors, because it *walks through walls*.

III.

This true attention, given to objects,
unerringly reveals the *presence of others*.

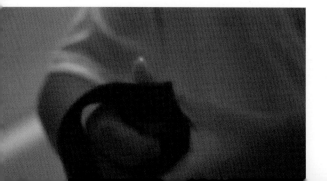

IV.

True attention allows potentialities latent in human relations and encounters — often immediately stifled by the weight of the everyday and by the hegemony of what is agreed to exist and to require attention — to flower and to flourish.

Attention nourishes the implicit forms of being together that are emergent within human interaction and that are constantly interrupted.

V.

An attentional path is the trace left by a free mind.
To *submit* to the attentional path of another, to
retrace it, is a form of attention.

Retracing the attentional path of a free mind is one of the keenest pleasures we can take in each other and in the world.

VI.

In this sense we must recognize a dialectic of attentional freedom: true attention consists in the ability to submit one's attention to the attentional path traced by another.

The absence of freedom of attention may thus feel like freedom (endless solicitation).

Freedom of attention may feel like unfreedom (deliberate submission).

VII.

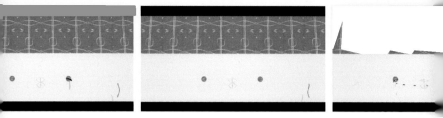

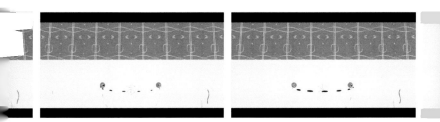

This dialectic has been deliberately manipulated by market structures and technologies to the point that we are *increasingly incapable of true attention*. Our attention has never been more free, or more continuously entrapped. Our attentional environments are thus *catastrophic*.

True attention is fundamentally *endangered*.

VIII.

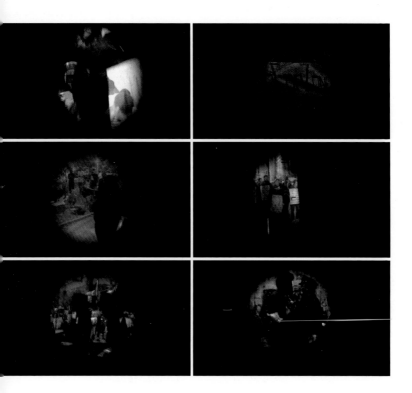

Escape from our attentional nightmare will not unfold in a singular event. The exercise of a truer attention requires the carving out of spaces in the world where it can survive and thrive — new environments.

This might manifest literally through the creation of spaces that facilitate new ways of gathering, but it also requires that we strengthen the relationship between our inner lives and our outer lives.

Sharing our individual sensory experiences with others is a means of reconciling a world that is otherwise broken. A world, that is, in which our ability to think for ourselves and to desire on our own terms is consistently threatened.

IX.

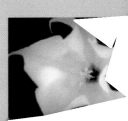

"Sanctuaries" of this sort for true attention *already exist*. They are among us now.

But they are endangered, and thus many are in hiding, operating in self-sustaining, inclusive, generous, and fugitive forms.

These sanctuaries can be found, but it takes an effort of attention to find them, and this seeking is also attention's effort to heal itself.

This *attention-which-seeks* often takes the form of an intense and near-devotional expectation and anticipation that refuses to know what it expects and anticipates.

X.

What is needed is an *ethics of attention*.
This is akin to a practical mysticism.

Practical mysticism is not impractical.
It is no more and no less than the
effort to draw closer to the astonishing
reality of things, through those forms of
pure attention that are unmixed with
evaluations of utility and judgment, and
free from the deforming grasp of a
seizing hand (or eye or mind).

XI.

True attention takes the unlivable and makes it livable. It is a lung that replenishes the air it breathes. If suddenly you feel that you can live and breathe in the place where you are, you or someone around you has committed, enacted, or bestowed attention.

This is our work.

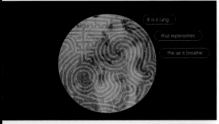

XII.

This work is the work of freedom and understanding.
It is a work, through attention, of world-building.

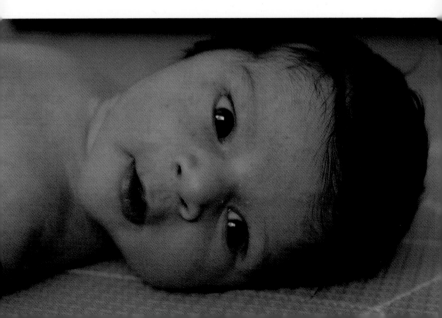

This work is fundamentally political.

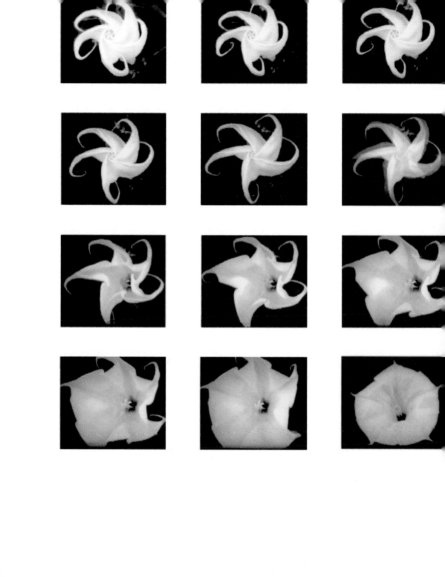

ACKNOWLEDGMENTS

The material presented in this book is the work of more than three dozen collaborators, each of whom stands in an individual and particular relation to any given image or sentence. Collaboration of this sort, when it works, is a little like a circus: lots of movement, many faces and voices, chaos and fun and a certain amount of drama. Just like the circus, people come and go — and there is lots of setup to do beforehand (and plenty of cleanup after)! A few words of acknowledgment, then, and thanks. The original draft of the *Twelve Theses* took shape at "The Politics of Attention: Art, Time, and Technology," held in 2019 at Mildred's Lane, the special retreat/colony on the New York – Pennsylvania border created by J. Morgan Puett and Mark Dion. Princeton University offered financial support for that workshop. Core contributors included: Kyle Berlin, D. Graham Burnett, Justin Ginsberg, Catherine Hansen, Adam Jasper, Stevie Knauss, Alyssa Loh, Anna Riley, and Matthew Strother. Key subsequent critical conversations/readings included: Daphne Barile, Grace Caiazza, Jeff Dolven, Leonard Nalencz, Jac Mullen, Jared Rankin, David Richardson, Hermione Spriggs, Emmet Stackelberg, and Caitlin Sweeney. In 2020/2021, Lane Stroud and Alyssa Loh collaborated with ten other remarkable filmmakers to create the set of *Twelve Theses* shorts that screened at the Glasgow International, and from which the stills in this book have been drawn. Those artists (and their respective Theses) are: 1. Izik Alequin; 2. Kevin Vu; 3. Terrance Daye; 4. Gianna Badiali; 5. Sofia Camargo Hoyos; 6. Alyssa Loh; 7. Pablo Chea; 8. Carman Spoto; 9. Amanda Gutiérrez; 10. Claudia Claremi; 11. Masami Kubo; 12. Lane Stroud. The sense of urgency that gave rise to all of this work had its spark in 2018 at the "Practices of Attention" symposium of the 33rd Bienal de São Paulo and the nexus of artists, scholars, activists, curators, and writers who participated in that project — not to mention the audiences who engaged with it. Special appreciation here goes to Gabriel Pérez-Barreiro and Stefanie Hessler. Without the support of Christie Henry and Marla Dirks, this book would not have found its way into your hands. Gratitude to all! A final word: the beautiful sequence of images depicting the *anthesis* of a night-blooming moonflower (*Ipomoea alba*) is the work of Jared Rankin. "The bud stands for all things..."